The Splendor of Love

BY DEAN WALLEY

ILLUSTRATED BY MYRON McVAY

♔

HALLMARK CROWN EDITIONS

....What is love?

....it is feeling, desire,

happiness,

   melancholy, contentment, sorrow,

    delight, inspiration, pleasure

....all words....and none of them

   can define

 the splendor of love.

....*but love*

shines out of the waters of earth....

....smiles out of its flower faces....

....murmurs in its winds of evening

....and we can hear love

in the varied voices

of nature.

Love is two rivers flashing proud
and free in the sun....darting down
the canyons of their youth
....until they meet.
Then mingling until two
are one....

....and the one broad river
flows slowly and peacefully on....
through tranquil valleys....

....*dreaming the one dream*

....*seeking the one sea*....

*Love is a reaching out....a
bringing together....
                    as the trees are earth's arms
embracing the sky....*

....as the sky is the cloak of

heaven, holding the earth

within its folds.

....In silent splendor, love

flows on endlessly

....seemingly without effect

....like water sliding over stone

....a transparent traveler over

faults and problems.

But just as water begins to leave

its mark....

so does love wear all the

rough places smooth.

Love is frail beauty
            ....like that of a butterfly
....so delicate and small....
                a pair of wings that weave
rainbows in the air....
        ....a captive of the wind.

Yet for all of its delicacy....

      the tiny butterfly can carry

            the blue sky on its back....

....and so love....

....the invisible force of the heart

....moves heaven and earth

to bring us joy....

Love can be a whirlwind....

a power that blows a path through the

wilderness that stands in our way....

....and it can be a gentle breeze

....bringing peace in the evening

....rocking a cradle

....renewing a life....

....and love is a seed

....from which only love can grow....

....transforming a barren life

into a garden of loveliness....

Like the miracle of dawn....the

herald of a new day....

....love is the enchanted dawn

of the heart....

....the bursting forth of light

out of darkness....

....and like the turning earth

....the revolving seasons....

love is a perfect circle....

....spiraling in ascending splendor

....within us

....all around us.

With no beginning

....with no ending....

.........*Love is always*.........

This book was designed and illustrated
by Myron McVay and David Welty.
The artists made their own color separations
and closely supervised the printing
for utmost accuracy of reproduction.
The type is set in Shakespeare Italic,
a typeface designed by Hermann Zapf
exclusively for Hallmark.
The paper is Hallclear, White Imitation Parchment
and Ivory Fiesta Parchment.
The cover is bound with imported
natural Seta silk book cloth and Torino paper.